101 No Frills Relationship Lessons You Need to Learn Before You Marry

Emmanuel Ogunjumo

Copyright © 2019

101 No Frills Relationship Lessons You Need to Learn Before You Marry
Copyright © 2019
Emmanuel Ogunjumo

All Rights Reserved by author Emmanuel Ogunjumo and printed in the United States of America. This book or parts thereof may not be reproduced in any form, stored in a retrieval system, or transmitted in any form by any means - electronic, mechanical, photocopy, recording or otherwise- without the prior written permission of the publisher, except as provided by the United States of America copyright law. Unless otherwise noted, all Scriptures quotations are from the Holy Bible, New International Version (2011) published by Zondervan Press used with permission.

Publisher: Absolute Author Publishing House
Editor: Dr. Melissa Caudle
Prayer Author: Dr. Melissa Caudle
Cover Designer: Rebecca Covers

Library of Congress Cataloging-in-Publication Data

Ogunjumo, Emmanuel

No Frills Relationship Lessons You Need to Learn Before You Marry/
Emmanuel Ogunjumo
p. cm.

ISBN: 978-1-951028-05-3

1. Religious   2. Self-help   3. Christian Marriage

---

0 1 2 3 4 5 6 7 8 9

Dedication

To my wonderful wife and eternal love.

Acknowledgments

There are many people whom I owe my gratitude in making this book a reality. First, to my wife for staying by my side and supporting me.

I would be remised if I didn't thank my editor from Absolute Author Publishing House, Dr. Melissa Caudle, for her expertise in editing and designing the interior of my book. Not only is she an exceptional editor, but she is also an author with many best-selling novels, including *Never Stop Running* and *A.D.A.M. The Beginning of Life*. She brought a unique perspective to this book as a licensed minister who authored each prayer at the end the chapters enhancing the message I presented. I can't thank her enough.

Table of Contents

Adam: Always Put God First 1

Cain: Your Relationship is Not a Competition 5

Sarah: It is Important to Forgive 9

Moses: Make Sure You are Equally Yoked 13

Eliezer: Don't Settle for Just Anybody 17

Isaac: Manage Your Expectations 21

Ruth: Position Yourself to Be Married 25

Nicodemus: What is Love? 30

Naaman: Find Love Despite Your Hang-ups 34

Apostle Peter's Wife: How to Deal with Disagreements 38

Mary's Husband Joseph: Think Twice Before Ending Your Relationship Over Bad News 42

Boaz: Look Beyond the Surface 46

David: Do Not Marry for Security 50

David: Set Boundaries 55

Leah: How to Survive a Stale Marriage 60
Hosea: It's Not About You 65
Job: Choose Wisely 70
Samson: Avoid This Mistake When Choosing 74
Vashti: Involve God and Wait on God's Timing 79
Solomon: Do Not Tolerate What is Wrong 83
Rachel: No One Can Make You Happy 87
Summary of Lessons 90
Summary of Scriptures 99
About the Author 103
Contact the Author 104

Adam
Always Put God First

I did not believe in love at first sight until I met her. Without a doubt, God outdid Himself when He created such beauty. Eve was like nothing I had ever seen before. I was awe-struck by her appearance, and the first word out of my mouth was "Wow ...man." So, I dropped the center W and called her, "Woman," as a tribute. I was love drunk, and both she and I knew it. I remember those early days fondly. They were absolutely wonderful!

Those days did not last. The wonder gradually went by the wayside the day we both decided to eat the fruit God told us not to eat. I will never forget that day. It was the day I abdicated responsibility for eating the fruit and instead threw Eve under the bus and blaming her for giving me the fruit in the first place.

At that moment, I completely neglected the fact that I possessed my free will and chose to eat the fruit.

Why did I eat that fruit you ask? I can't point to just one reason, but a couple of ideas come to my mind. First, the red fruit looked delicious and appetizing. Second, I knew she desired the fruit too. So, I thought, why not? I convinced myself that not only was I going to please my wife, but also by eating it, we would move forward to our goal of becoming one. I reasoned to myself that God wouldn't mind us disobeying His word since it would help us fulfill His desire for us becoming one in His eyes.

What is that popular saying people have today? Ahh yes, "Happy wife, happy life." It didn't quite work out that way for us. When I ate the fruit, Eve was happy in that instant, but her temporary feeling quickly faded. It did not take us long to realize we had opened a Pandora's box of hurt in our relationship. Our happiness promptly disappeared, and our lives became miserable.

The immediate period of adjustment to our new normal was especially rough. After experiencing marital Heaven for so long, our new normal seemed like marital Hell. We pointed fingers toward each other and had many horrible arguments. Instead of us becoming closer to each other, eating the forbidden fruit ended up separating us. Why did we eat the fruit? We asked ourselves that question many times. The taste was certainly not worth the pain. Why did we not listen to God? His instructions were self-explanatory. "Don't eat the fruit!"

I am grateful that Eve and I committed to our marriage. As time passed, we both realized that we must let go of the past to move forward. Neither of us could go back in time and fix our mistakes, although we desired it. We had to make the best of our situation and learn from our past mistakes. God allowed us to do that. Clearly, we would not have been in our predicament if only we had listened to God. From that moment, we stopped debating whether to believe God or not. We realized He was infinitely wiser than we would ever be and so we submitted to His lordship, His instructions, His commands, and His leading. It is never too late for you to do the same.

Relationship Lessons

1. Never sacrifice permanent joy for temporary gratification; the taste is not worth the pain.
2. God knows what is best for your relationship – always listen to Him and obey the commands He has for you.
3. You must let go of the past wrongs to move forward in your relationship with God and with your future or current spouse.
4. Your commitment to God will bolster your commitment to your partner
5. Your relationship will be exceptional if you are both committed to God in all things and remain faithful to His will and plans for you both.

Meditation and Prayer

Trust in the LORD with all your heart, and do not rely on your own understanding **– Proverbs 3:5 -**

Dear Lord, I lift my praise up to you because You are worthy. I ask that You bless me today and my relationship and lead me in Your ways so that Your will be done according to your plan. I ask for Your forgiveness for my wrongs and open my heart to Your word. In Jesus' name, I pray. Amen.

Life Application

How can you use the lessons learned in this chapter and apply it to your relationship? Meditate on your answer and lift up your specific prayer to God. He is faithful, and He will deliver.

Cain
Your Relationship is Not a Competition

I knew better, but I did not do better! I have no excuses for my thoughts or my behavior. My dad warned me that God's commandments should never be broken and that I must adhere to them. I remember his words even now. As I was growing up, Adam said to me, "Son, the commands God has given us are not there to prevent us from enjoying the best life, they are there to protect us from experiencing the worst life."

I knew I should have offered the first fruit of the land to God, but I didn't. I reasoned that since I worked hard for the harvest, I should enjoy the first produce from the land and I conveniently chose to forget that as the landowner, God was the owner of all things harvested from it. I forgot about how generous He was to allow me to keep all that was produced on His land except the first fruits. So, I took His generosity for granted and purposefully withheld what I knew was His.

What happened next is like what happened when Homer Simpson gave Marge Simpson a bowling ball for her birthday although she had never bowled a day in her life. God was displeased, and He rejected my offering.

Instead of accepting responsibility for what happened, I became furious. I turned my anger toward my brother, knowing it was futile to be angry at God. As I focused all my ire toward Abel, God intervened to warn me that my feelings were getting the best of me. He warned me that my anger was quickly approaching the point of no return.

Rather than heed His warnings, I filled my heart with thoughts of how I felt about the things Abel should have done. I convinced myself that he could have offered me some of his firstborn animals. Did he? No! He could have cautioned me not to offer up just any portion of the fruits. Did he? No! He could have pleaded with God to accept my offering, but he didn't do that too.

I believed that I was the victim of Abel's competitive spirit. I convinced myself that he did not do any of the things he could have done because he wanted me to look like a fool in front of God. He wanted to show God that he was better than me. I reasoned that he was happy inside and snickering at my shame. I made him the enemy and blamed him for my shortcomings, never accepting responsibility for my actions.

As I walked around, seething with anger, I suddenly heard a small voice whisper to me. "Cain, if you can't do better than the competition, why don't you just get rid of the competition." It was precisely what my fragile ego wanted to hear. So, I did the unthinkable and got rid of Abel, permanently! Yes, I killed him.

Looking back, it is clear that I let my anger take me over the edge. I should have allowed my anger and frustrations to pass. I should have listened to wise counsel, but I didn't. I let my negative emotions get the better of me, influence my decisions, and I lived to regret it.

Maybe like me, you have let your competitive spirit get out of hand. Maybe, you can't stand the thought of being wrong or criticized by others. Remember, that by definition, for someone to win, someone must lose. Your relationship should be a win-win situation. For that to happen, you must focus on community and not competition.

Remember that if you insist on your rights, your relationship will throw you some lefts to go with the rights.

Relationship Lessons

1. Don't take your relationship with God for granted.
2. Maintain an attitude of gratitude; it will keep you from a lot of trouble.
3. Accept responsibility for your mess-ups instead of trying to justify them or blame them on others.
4. Look for and pay attention to the wise counsel of others.
5. Any decision you make when you're angry and frustrated will only hurt you and your relationship.

6. Look to live in community with one another instead of in competition.

Meditation and Prayer

If you become angry, do not let your anger lead you into sin, and do not stay angry all day. — **Ephesians 4:26** —

Dear Heavenly Father, I come to you broken and with a competitive spirit. I know that I have messed-up and made terrible decisions. I ask for Your mercy and grace to grant me release of my competitiveness so that I may shine bright to do Your will. I pray that I take responsibility for my actions and not blame others. I praise Your holy name. Amen.

Life Application

How can you use the lessons learned in this chapter and apply it to your relationship? Meditate on your answer and lift up your specific prayer to God. He is faithful and He will deliver.

Sarah
It is Important to Forgive

I couldn't believe it! I wondered what could have happened to my bold and courageous husband.

Just a few months before, Abram stood in front of me, declaring that we had to leave our family and friends because God wanted us to go! When I asked where, he said, "I don't know. All he knew was that we had to do it. Although I had my doubts about whether he had really heard from God or had just experienced a rush of blood to the head, I agreed to go with him.

Why did I do it? I agreed because I loved him, respected him, and wanted to honor his leadership of our family. You see, I am a bride in the traditional mold.

Now in Canaan, I wondered if I had made the right decision to follow him. Trust me; I had my doubts. The man standing in front of me was no longer bold and assured but looked like a wet puppy dog. He was so afraid for his life that he asked me to lie and tell others that I was his sister. Nope, not his fiancé, not even his girlfriend, but his sister! Can you imagine my hurt and the betrayal I felt?

Although I remained calm on the outside, I was boiling inside! What happened to 'till death do us part'? What happened to commitment? What happened to 'have faith in God'? Fear replaced my faith; cowardice replaced my courage, and selfishness replaced my selflessness. Needless to say, I was torn and an emotional wreck.

I nearly lost my respect for him that day, and I would have lost it but for an inner voice that spoke to me at the right moment. "Just because he is making a mistake does not mean his decision to leave was a mistake."

The words were profound to me, and at that moment, I realized that the man making this decision was an ugly caricature of the man I knew and loved. So, I made a conscious decision to respect him despite having zero respect for his decision to call me his sister. I chose not to evaluate our relationship solely on what he did wrong.

Over the years, the question I get asked the most is why I agreed to his request to say I was his sister. The reasons were two-fold. First, I thought that he would come to his senses sooner rather than later and declare to everyone that I was his wife. Second, I knew God had a plan and purpose for our lives, which was much bigger than both of us combined.

It was the second reason that gave me the courage to face my dilemma. Although Abram had failed me, I knew God never goes back on his word. Indeed, if Abram were faithless, God would remain faithful! How could I go wrong with that? I wrapped myself up in my faith.

Looking back, I am so grateful that God keeps His promises. I say this because Abram did not come to his senses immediately. Instead, he asked me to lie about being his sister a second time! Are you kidding me? If not for God's hand, our marriage would have been over!

However, to be fair, Abram was not the only one that made mistakes in our marriage. After many years of waiting for our child, I became fearful that it would not happen. So, I started to second guess what I knew. I said to myself, "When God said Abram would have a child, perhaps God did not mean he would have a child with me." Maybe He meant Abram would have a child with someone else. I convinced myself so much of this lie that I decided to help God out. I asked Abram to sleep with my maidservant. How silly is that! Just as Abram's decision almost cost us our marriage, my decision almost cost us our marriage.

Relationship Lessons

1. For your relationship to last, you must look past what is wrong with your partner and instead focus on what is right with your partner.
2. It is not a matter of if you must forgive each other, it is a matter of when you must forgive.
3. Being disappointed in any relationship is inevitable but being discouraged is a choice.

4. Fear makes terrible relationship decisions, so never make any decisions out of fear.
5. Keep your focus on God's promises when going through a rough patch.

Meditation and Prayer

If we are faithless, He remains faithful; He cannot deny Himself. **– 2 Timothy 2:13 –**

Dear Heavenly Father, I ask first for Your forgiveness for all my trespasses against You and those I love. Please help me to accept that decisions will be made by others that impact my life and to guide me to accept them according to Your will. I ask that you give me the strength and courage to look past the faults of others, especially in my partner, and to find the good within them that You blessed them. When disappointment comes my way, help me to remain steadfast in my faith and to turn everything over to You and not to decide out of fear or in anger. You above all can answer my prayer, and I lift these up to you in praise of Your name. In Jesus name, Amen.

Life Application

How can you use the lessons learned in this chapter and apply it to your relationship? Meditate on your answer and lift up your specific prayer to God. He is faithful and He will deliver.

Moses
Make Sure You Are Equally Yoked

How I met Zipporah is exciting and is the stuff movie producers love to film. I was a fugitive on the run, high tailing it from Egypt! I didn't have a choice. I could have stayed to face the executioner's ax, or I could take my chances with the robbers, raiders, serpents, and scorpions. I chose the latter. Therefore, I ended up in the desert, hungry, thirsty, and half delirious.

Many thoughts ran through my head. Where would I get the next meal and drink? Would anyone show me mercy and take me into their home? Had I made the right decision to leave Egypt? I was beginning to reason that the executioner's ax would have been much swifter than this slow death in the middle of nowhere.

Then I saw it, an oasis in the distance. For once, it wasn't a mirage. In front of me were seven ladies and a few men, but I couldn't make out what was happening. I slowly approached, trying to gauge the situation, and practiced in my head what I would say. I needed the right words so they would invite me in to rest without asking too many questions.

As fate would have it, I didn't need any of those words. Those men were not friends, but foes. They were unwelcomed raiders. I took it as an opportunity to make a great impression. I sprang into action and thankfully succeeded in driving them away. I became an instant hero! That act of heroism not only won me a stay at the oasis, but it also helped win over Zipporah's heart.

Zipporah and I were happy. I went from being a fugitive to having a family. She went from being alone to having a man who could not leave her alone. Then came the day I met God. As I grew closer to Him and learned of His purpose for me, Zipporah and I grew further apart. It wasn't her fault. She never changed; I did. She didn't understand God's purpose for me. To her, we had a good life. We were safe, secure, and had our family close to us. She wondered what type of a God would want to take that away from those He loved? Why would God put those he claimed to love in that path of peril? She didn't know God the way I knew Him. In fact, she did not know God at all. She only knew about Him. So, whereas I was filled with faith and hope, she was filled with fear and doubt.

Rather than focus on introducing her to God, I focused on calming her fears. That was a mistake. No matter how many times her fears went away, they always returned. Still, she reluctantly agreed to go back to Egypt with me. She loved me too much and did not want our family to be separated. Her only condition was that she get to know God first before introducing Him to our children. I agreed! I was positive that everything would change as she got to know God as I did. To honor our agreement, I did not circumcise our boys as God instructed me to do. That was another mistake. I almost lost my life because of it.

That whole experience was an eye-opener. I learned that God instructs us to keep us from unforeseen danger, and I learned that Zipporah was not sold on God at all. She circumcised the boys to save my life, but she was furious that she had to. She was mad at both God and me. There is nothing like a woman's fury. Although we went to Egypt together, we didn't leave Egypt together. She didn't like Egypt, did not believe in God or what I was doing and thought I was putting our family in danger for no reason. Therefore, she left with the boys.

It wasn't until God delivered the slaves out of Egypt under my leadership, did she come to believe in God and in me. By that time, our marriage was broken and beyond the point of no return.

Relationship Lessons

1. You are setting yourself up for a rude awakening if you expect you or your partner never to change.
2. The key to maintaining your relationship is making sure you change together.

3. It is not enough that you love each other; it is vital that you share the same vision for your lives. Having two visions leads to division.
4. It is better, to be honest, and truthful at the start rather than go along with something you know you can't handle.
5. Make sure you fix any serious issues you may have before introducing any major life changes.

Meditation and Prayer

*Can two walk together, unless they are agreed? – **Amos 3:3**–*

My Heavenly Father, grant me the ability to accept those around me for who they are and not to try to change them into whom I want them to be. You are the designer and creator of life, and I accept that you made each one of us as we are for Your glory and Your purpose. I ask that You help me to see the plan You have for me so that I may serve and bring glory to Your name. And, I ask that I share the same vision with my partner as we serve You. In Your humble service, I ask these things in Jesus' name. Amen.

Life Application

How can you use the lessons learned in this chapter and apply it to your relationship? Meditate on your answer and lift up your specific prayer to God. He is faithful and He will deliver.

Eliezer
Don't Settle for Just Anybody

Abraham knew very well that outside of our decision to choose God, our most significant decision in life is whom we decide to marry. So, he decided he was not going to compromise on the qualities he wanted in a wife for his son. Seeing that no one matched the qualities he was looking for in Canaan, he decided to look outside of the city.

Before I left to fulfill his wish, he gave me two specific instructions. First, he told me to go to his kinsmen. I didn't understand why he was so particular about that until I thought about it further. He and his kinsmen had one thing in common -- they are related by blood. Today, those who have accepted Christ into their hearts have entered the family of God and are related to each other by the blood of Jesus. Therefore, if you are going to choose someone to marry, make sure they belong to your spiritual family.

Second, he told me Isaac was not to leave Canaan even if his bride would not leave her land. When he told me this, I realized that his desire for obeying God was more significant to him than his desire to see his son married. He put God first and understood that Isaac was in the place of his promise. He knew that taking Isaac away from Canaan to be married would have resulted in temporary happiness; however, it would have been at the expense of fulfilling his purpose and destiny. That was too high a cost!

When I got to my destination, I dropped to my knees in prayer and asked for favor and wisdom. I didn't want to look only with physical eyes but with spiritual eyes as well. I wanted a woman who would be hard-working, caring, considerate, and loving. I wanted a good woman; I wanted a godly woman for Isaac.

Shortly after my prayer, I saw a stunningly beautiful woman approaching the well. Wondering how she could still be single; I quickly ran over to her to start a conversation. When I asked her for a drink of water, she immediately considered my camels. She said she would draw water for them without me having to say as much as a word about it.

As I watched her go back and forth to draw water from the well for my camels, I wondered if she was Abraham's kin. As God would have it, she was! So, I quickly brought out the bracelet I had on me and placed it on her wrist. At last, I found a bride for Isaac.

Relationship Lessons

1. Do not compromise your values – if you can't find what you are looking for in one place, expand your search. Do not limit yourself to one country, one ethnicity, one culture.
2. Do not yoke yourself to anyone that does not belong to your spiritual family.
3. Do not make the goal of being married more important than obeying God – any marriage that takes you away from fulfilling your purpose and destiny should be avoided.
4. Ask God for favor, wisdom, and spiritual eyes to see before choosing a potential spouse.
5. Do not delay in making a move when you see someone you like & do not delay 'putting a ring on it' when you know that person is the one for you.

Meditation and Prayer

Don't become partners with those who do not believe. For what partnership is there between righteousness and lawlessness? Or what fellowship does light have with darkness? **– 2 Corinthians 6:14 –**

Dear merciful Father, I come to you with a humble heart to ask that you guide me in selecting my life-long partner who will compliment me under Your banner and that we share the same values and beliefs that will bring glory to You. I know that you have created the perfect partner for me so that we may serve You. I ask that You give me favor, wisdom, and spiritual eyes to recognize my potential spouse. Blessed is Your name, and I pray these things in Jesus' name. Amen.

Life Application

How can you use the lessons learned in this chapter and apply it to your relationship? Meditate on your answer and lift up your specific prayer to God. He is faithful and He will deliver.

Isaac
Manage Your Expectations

I was forty years old and unmarried! It wasn't because there were no suitors for me, there were plenty. My father, Abraham, was an extremely wealthy and respected man for God had favored him. Therefore, every 'who was who in the zoo' brought their daughter to our house hoping they'd find favor in my father's eyes. They desired to yoke their family to ours, knowing they would be financially set if they joined their family to ours. Father knew this, so he kept turning them down. He said to me, "Son, I want to make sure that the person who marries you is not just doing it for your inheritance."

So, year after year, my father kept turning down all the prospects that came to our house. When he saw that I was becoming restless, he sat me down and told me it was better to wait on God's timing than rush into an ill-advised union, and he did assure me that God would provide.

Who was I to argue? I was born when my parents were beyond their seventies and had seen how my father's obedience to God and patience brought him many blessings. Although I did not quite have my father's faith, I trusted in his faith in God. What I didn't consider was that my father was also watching me closely. He waited to see if I was ready to take up the mantle of marriage. He decided I was ready when I reached the age of forty.

When the time came, he decided to send Eliezer out of Canaan and back to his home country -- a place I had never been. Apparently, he determined that everyone in our country desired to be joined to our family for the wrong reasons.

It was certainly not what I thought would happen. I had my heart set on finding someone close to home.

Knowing that Eliezer acted as God led him, and knowing that God knows best, I welcomed Rebekah with open arms and received her as my wife. Married life was sweet until we discovered Rebekah was barren.

Rather than get mad at God, I recalled how God had opened my mother's womb, Sarah, to have me.

So, I strengthened myself, saying, "If God answered my parent's prayers after so many years of asking for a child, He will answer my prayers too."

In this second waiting season, God taught me two valuable lessons. First, just because I am in the will of God doesn't mean everything in my life will go smoothly. Second, just because dreadful things happen, it doesn't mean I am out of the will of God, or those terrible things are part of God's will.

Twenty years after our marriage, God opened Rebekah's womb. It just goes to show that delay is not denial.

Relationship Lessons

1. Marry only when you are ready. It is better to be married later in life than to marry early and have a miserable marriage that ends in divorce.
2. Settle only for a quality spouse – No matter how many men and women there are, you will be with only one. Hearing a lot of 'no's' does not mean you are on the wrong track.
3. Be open to the person God desires for you. Having an idea of the person you desire to be with is fine but be open to the possibility of God moving you in a different direction.
4. Married life is not always a bouquet of flowers. Just because you are in the will of God does not mean everything in your marriage will go smoothly.
5. No waiting period is ever wasted. God always has a lesson in the waiting period. Look for it.
6. Pray and be patient through your troubles. When issues do pop up, remain prayerful, and ask God to grant you the wisdom to know how to wait. Delay is not denial.

Meditation

*Be still and know that I am God. – **Psalm 46:10** –*

Dear Lord, I come to you with open arms and filled with Your spirit. I am anxious and feel impatient, which I know does not bring glory to Your name. I ask that you give me the wisdom to recognize that Your timing is not my timing and that You perform Your miracles according to the plans You have for me. Although I do not like to wait on Your answers, I accept that You have Your reasons. I ask that you guide me in the wisdom to learn how to wait and be still to hear You speak to me. In all things in Your glory, I pray. In Jesus' name, I lift my request to you. Amen.

Life Application

How can you use the lessons learned in this chapter and apply it to your relationship? Meditate on your answer and lift up your specific prayer to God. He is faithful and He will deliver.

Ruth
Position Yourself to Be Married

If there was any woman who did not have any hope of getting married, it was me. My first husband was dead. I did not have a penny to my name, and I was going to a land where the men of the area did not welcome people, especially women, from my country. If you are wondering why, let me give a brief history lesson.

A few hundred years back, women from my country, Moab, were sent to the men of Israel to seduce them with sex and idolatry. The proposition was something like this. "I will only allow you to get some of this (sex) if you turn and worship my idol."

This proposition was part of a strategy executed by the king of Moab to keep Israel weak because he was afraid his enemies would conquer him. The king was told that if the men turned away from God, God would not favor them. The strategy worked!

Many battle-hardened men slept with our women, and those men were slain. Since that time, Israel looked at people from Moab with much suspicion, especially the women.

I was sure no man would be interested in a newly converted Moabite. What was I going to say to any man? "Hey handsome, I am from Moab. I am new here. My mother-in-law and I came here after my husband died and because we heard there was food here. Oh, I have recently turned away from my idols and converted to Judaism, so you don't have to worry about that. One more thing, I don't have a penny to my name. Would you like to go on a date?"

With the odds stacked against me, I put the idea of marriage far away from my thinking, although I secretly desired it. Instead, I focused my attention on providing for my mother-in-law and me. This I did by going from field to field, day after day, picking up any leftovers the ground keepers were kind enough to leave behind for us to eat and to survive.

At first, others left me to be alone in these fields, and then they began to warm up to me as they witnessed my industry, tested my character, and learned of my story. One day soon after, I happened upon a field owned by Boaz. I collected more grain in his field than I had ever collected in any other. I was grateful for his kindness but thought no more of it.

Thankfully my mother-in-law was more discerning than I was. She explained to me that it was unusual to come home with such substantial amounts of grain. She suggested that Boaz must have taken an interest in me. I said to her, "If indeed he has taken an interest in me, then why hasn't he pursued that interest? Why hasn't he mentioned something to me?"

My mother-in-law laughed at my immature thinking. She explained that there were men who do not pursue their interest in fear of rejection. She said, "You know how successful and well-respected Boaz is in the community. I am sure many women have been interested in him, and I am sure he has been interested in other women, but I bet those other women waited for him to approach them and pursue his interest in them. After waiting for too long, these ladies felt rejected or thought of him as an unserious element. They might have even thought he was not interested in marriage."

Poor women! They waited for him to act in line with cultural norms and tradition, but he never did.

Then she added, "Ruth, don't be like the other women. He has shown interest in you. Now you must leave no doubt in his mind that you are extremely interested. He is the kind of man that does not take hints well. You have to pursue the interest he has shown in you."

Scared and fighting against fear of rejection, I followed my mother-in-law's advice and showed him that I was available. Instead of finding my actions desperate, he found it desirable. It gave him the confidence to pursue marriage.

I later found out that he had been inquiring about me and thought the world of me. If I had not listened to my mother-in-law's advice, and if I had not decided to do something out of my comfort zone, I am not sure I would have gotten married.

If you are a woman that desires to be married, there is hope. If I could end up married with the odds stacked against me, then you can too. However, I want you to understand that there is no pre-defined process to follow. Get rid of any picture you may have conjured in your heart about how it is going to happen.

Whether he pursues you or you pursue him is inconsequential. The only thing that matters is that you are both interested in each other and that you both give consent.

Furthermore, don't let church tradition and diverse cultural norms get in your way. Feel free to break the rules without breaking God's laws and principles. Remember, even Jesus broke many man-made religious rules without breaking God's laws and principles while pursuing us.

Relationship Lessons

1. Don't allow the things you can't do anything about stop you from pursuing your desire to marry. When the right person comes along, he won't care about things such as whether you were previously married, have kids, how old you are, etc.
2. Not every person is comfortable pursuing a relationship. If you are interested, you may have to make the first sure move.
3. There is no full-proof process to follow to get into a relationship and get married. The most important thing is to make sure that you choose wisely.

4. If you desire to be married, make sure you put your best foot forward. Moreover, remember this, if things don't work out, that there is no such thing as rejection, there is only redirection.
5. Sometimes you must break with culture and traditions to get what you desire. Don't let those stop you if you are not breaking God's commandments.

Meditation and Prayer

Who are you? he asked. "It's Ruth, sir," she answered. Because you are a close relative, you are responsible for taking care of me. So please marry me. **– Ruth 3:9 –**

Dear Precious Lord, I come to you with fear in my heart that I may never find the right partner to live out the rest of my days. I know I shouldn't worry, but I do. I pray that You find me worthy of Your grace and guide me in the right direction. Please show me the way and grant me discernment to know when I have found the one who will fulfill Your purpose for us in marriage. May you grant me an open heart to rid any prejudices that I harbor and accept the differences in others. In Jesus' name, I bring forth my requests to honor You. Amen.

Life Application

How can you use the lesson learned in this chapter and apply it to your relationship? Meditate on your answer and lift up your specific prayer to God. He is faithful and He will deliver.

Nicodemus
What is Love?

I thought I knew what I believed until I heard Jesus speak. After listening to his words, I was not sure anymore. Although I tried to dismiss His teachings, I couldn't because of the miracles he continued to perform. How could anyone doubt Him after that?

Unable to take it any longer, I decided to visit Him under cover of the night. I knew I was taking an elevated risk by visiting Him, but I did it anyway. I needed answers to my questions! The risk was worth the reward.

He spoke many things that I did not understand that night, and one particular statement he made about love, struck me to my core. He said, "For God so loved the world that He gave His only begotten Son, that whosoever believes in Him will not perish but have everlasting life."

I thought more about His words as I walked home that night.

"For God so loved the world..." The word world stuck with me. Why did God love the world? What did the world do to deserve such love? Shouldn't He punish the world? As these thoughts ran throughout my head, I had an epiphany. Love is not a reward but a gift. It is based solely on the heart of the giver and not on the performance of the receiver. While a reward can be earned, a gift can only be received. I realized that if someone must deserve my love, then it is not love at all. I could not escape this truth -- my ability to love depends solely on the condition of my heart.

"That he gave his only begotten Son..." This part made me realize that love demands action. Love just doesn't talk about meeting a need; it does something to meet the need. Furthermore, love positions itself to give rather than receive. Also, it is not looking to give just anything; it is looking to give its absolute best. This is what God did with His Son. Therefore, it is what I should do as well if I truly have love in my heart.

I realized that love gives its absolute best to meet the needs of those who are not deserving. This made me think about how I love those in my care. Do I treat them differently depending on their behavior? Do I always give my best no matter what?

"That whosoever believes in Him..." That He used the word whosoever told me that not everybody accepts love. Just because I selflessly sacrifice to meet the needs of others, does not mean my love will be accepted. This was a hard pill to swallow.

It showed me that love does not expect a reward for its actions. It also taught me that love is not always a bed of roses. It can involve degrees of disappointment and pain. People may question my motivation for choosing to love them. They might even reject it outright. Yet, I should love them, anyway.

"Will not perish but have everlasting life..." This part was beautiful to me. It warmed my heart to know that love succeeds in the end. Although I might go through the pain of rejection, the sacrifice will be worth it in the end. Love not only saves but it has a long-lasting effect in the lives of those who receive it.

By the time I arrived home, I had come up with two definitions for love. First, love is a selfless sacrifice to serve and meet the needs of others. Second, love is a determined action to lift people and give them the best life that they can possibly have.

When I reached home, I at once told my wife I loved her. This time I knew what I was saying and purposed in my heart to show her more of the love I professed.

Relationship Lessons

1. Love is not about getting your needs met first, it is first about meeting the needs of your partner.
2. When you say, "I love you," to someone, you should mean, "I selflessly sacrifice to serve you."
3. Love is not a feeling; love is an action.

4. Love is a gift given based on the heart of the giver and not a reward given based on the performance of the receiver.
5. Love is a committed expression to others of the love we have received from God.

Meditation and Prayer

For God so loved the world that He gave His only Begotten Son that whosoever believes in Him should not perish but have everlasting life. – John 3:16 –

Dear Lord, I want to thank You for loving sinners like me unconditionally. You set the standard and showed us the way; yet, we often fall short. I pray that You show me how to treat others as You treat them and to love my partner with the same unconditional love You have for us. I realize that to honestly love someone, I must make hard sacrifices and be selfless in all things. Please grant me Your grace, love, and mercy so that I may give unconditional love to bring glory to Your name. I am Your humble servant, and I ask these things in the name of Jesus. Amen.

Life Application

How can you use the lessons learned in this chapter and apply it to your relationship? Meditate on your answer and lift up your specific prayer to God. He is faithful and He will deliver.

Naaman
Find Love Despite Your Hang-ups

Have you ever heard someone say, "Why would anyone want to be with me? I am damaged goods. I carry too much baggage, and I will never find true love."

Maybe these words resonate with you because you have felt or currently feel that way. Perhaps you think this way because you are overweight. Maybe it's because you are divorced and are raising your kids. Or, perhaps because you have some deformity or disability.

If you feel this way, I want you to know you are not alone. I have been where you are. I was an up and coming military leader with a budding career. I had the king's ear and happily married to a stunningly beautiful woman. Then one day, I noticed a light-colored skin patch on my arm. Alarmed, I immediately went to the doctor where he confirmed I had leprosy!

There was no treatment for leprosy in those days. All who had the disease were quarantined. They were left to fend for themselves and became pariahs. Stunned and confused about what the doctor told me, I walked around town aimlessly. I didn't know how to break the news to my wife, family, or military superior. I thought about disappearing and walking away quietly from everything. I reasoned that it would be better for everyone concerned and I thought my life was over.

After this period of fear-filled thinking, my military training took over. I had been trained to face my battles, so that was what I decided to do. I went to my wife, family, and my superior and told them my diagnosis.

My superior immediately mentioned that no one gets left behind. He also mentioned that he thought I had a brilliant military mind and said it would be a shame to allow such a disease to ruin my ability to serve the country. Then he said these words that stuck with me, "Naaman, who you are is much greater than what you have."

My wife and family said something similar. They informed me that they wouldn't give up on me, and if this happened to anyone of them, they wouldn't give up on them either. I took comfort in the fact that my family would never leave me or give up on me.

I was overwhelmed by their support. At that moment, I realized that I had been telling myself a story about how people would respond to me. Although not everyone responded favorably to the news, the people who mattered and cared about me reacted positively.

In time, people forgot that I was leprous. I became the commander of the army and advised the king on all critical matters.

Moreover, my wife never gave up on me. She looked for anything or anyone who could help find a cure. Because of how she treated people, a house girl who had recently been forcibly removed from her household in a raid in Israel and brought to Syria to serve, my wife, took pity on her.

Think about how improbable that was. She told my wife about a prophet who performed many miracles and could possibly help heal my leprosy. Because of the way my wife treated this girl, I ended up meeting the prophet. He ended up curing my leprosy, and I ended up believing in God.

If you think my story is just Biblical folklore, consider the current example of Nick Vujicic, who was born without hands or legs. Today, he is a well-known international speaker who is married to a beautiful wife, who has hands and feet, and he is a father to three children. If Nick can overcome his disability to find love, who are you to despair about your situation?

Relationship Lessons

1. Give people a chance to love you because you are worthy just the way you are to be loved.
2. Don't disqualify yourself from love prematurely because of the stories you have told yourself.
3. Your good character toward people forges loyalty in their relationship with you.
4. Who you are as a person is more important to people compared to what you may or may not have.

5. The people that love you will not abandon you in your time of trouble.

Meditation and Prayer

*For as he (a man) thinks in his heart, so is he. – **Proverbs 23:7 –***

Dear Heavenly Father, I come to You in love with You, knowing that Your love is eternal. Thank you for creating me the way I am because I am Your child, and you created me exactly how You wanted. Please help me to accept my flaws so that I may bring honor and glory to You. You, above all else, knows and understands who I am and what I can do. Please guide me in Your ways as I am. In His name, I shout praise and glory for what You will do in me as I am. Amen.

Life Application

How can you use the lessons learned in this chapter and apply it to your relationship? Meditate on your answer and lift up your specific prayer to God. He is faithful, and He will deliver.

Emmanuel Ogunjumo

Apostle Peter's Wife
How to Deal with Disagreements

I was in the kitchen when my husband, Peter, came barging through the door. He was so excited that he could hardly get a word out. All he kept on saying was, "Look at this," as he dropped a money sack on the table.

I took a glance and immediately stepped back in fear. "Where did you get this money?" I said before I could help it. "Return it from wherever you took it."

My husband was a fisherman. I knew how much fishermen earned in a day, and he had brought home two week's wages in one day! Seeing that I was losing my mind, Peter quickly reassured me that he didn't do anything illegal to obtain the money.

Then he told me about his encounter with an odd man. He explained that after catching nothing all day long, he came across a guy who told him to cast his net one more time. For some reason, Peter, my typically rebellious husband, obeyed the man. To his surprise, he caught so much fish that he and his crew could hardly haul in the catch.

I hugged Peter, praised him for deciding not to be so stubborn, and inquired if he thanked the man. He responded by saying that not only did he thank the man, but the man gave him an offer to follow him. He then told me he accepted the offer. I was excited! I was thinking of all the fishing tricks and tips he could give Peter. Obviously, this man must be an expert fisherman. "What is the name of his fishing company?" I asked.

"No! No! No! You have the wrong idea," Peter responded. "He does not own a fishing company. I am not even sure if he has fished a day in his life. He is some kind of prophet. He asked me to give up my fishing business and follow him. He said that instead of being a fisherman, he'd make me a fisher of man. Fisherman... fisher of man... get it?"

I did not find his joke funny. I thought Peter lost his mind. Many thoughts ran through my head. "Who was this man? How were we going to survive without any income?"

I was scared and anxious. I had always supported Peter, but this was a bridge too far for me to travel. So, I told him, "No!"

We fought the entire day. He told me to have faith, and I told him to use his head. He responded that he would do what was in his heart. Realizing we were not getting anywhere, we decided to put some temporary distance between us.

He went for a walk, promising to consider my concerns. I sat down on the mat to allow my fears to abate. I knew Peter loved me and would do anything for our family. I knew that he must really believe in this man if he decided to go with him. I started to think of what I could do to help us make ends meet and considered how this would work. I started to look for solutions.

In the end, we decided to use both our heads and our hearts. Our hearts determined the destination, but our heads would lead the way to that destination. We reasoned that if he was truly a prophet, then we would not go hungry. If he were not the prophet, Peter would return to the fishing business. With this plan, I decided to support Peter in his decision. Though this was one of the scariest things I have had to do; yet, it ended up being the best decision of my life.

The man was indeed whom he said he was. We lacked for absolutely nothing, and he ended up healing my mother. The more time Peter spent with him, the more he changed. He became a better husband and a better person. It changed the course of his life and ended up helping to change the course of the history of man. I am glad he chose significance over security. I am also delighted I supported him.

Relationship Lessons

1. You must think for yourself instead of allowing your fears to think for you.
2. It is important to take a deliberate break to truly consider the other person's point of view.
3. You should consider both your head and heart when deciding. If you only allow your head to rule, it will take you to a place where your heart feels empty.

4. To make your partner more comfortable, give yourself an alternative solution in the event whatever decision you make does not work so well.
5. If you respond when you are -- Frustrated, Angry, Upset, Lonely, or Tired (F.A.U.L.T), then you are equally at fault for the argument.

Meditation and Prayer

> *A man's heart plans his way, but the Lord directs his steps.* **– Proverbs 16:9 –**
>
> *My dear precious Lord, please hear my prayer. I face many challenges and new beginnings which frighten me. I know that You cover me with Your banner and shield me; so, I have no reason to be fearful. Yet, I am. I pray that You will bring peace to me and guide me in my decisions to meet the challenges You put before me. I accept that You will not give me anything that I cannot handle because Your word is true and just. Thank you in advance for relieving me of my fear and doubts. In Your glorious name, I lift my requests to you. Amen.*

Life Application

How can you use the lessons learned in this chapter and apply it to your relationship? Meditate on your answer and lift up your specific prayer to God. He is faithful, and He will deliver.

Mary's Husband Joseph
Think Twice Before Ending Your Relationship Over Bad News

There is a saying, "If it looks like a duck, swims like a duck, and quacks like a duck, then it probably is a duck." The situation I found myself facing fit this saying perfectly. When Mary came to me and told me that she was pregnant, the case seemed closed. She cheated on me. There was no mystery to be solved, especially considering that we had not been physically intimate with one another. Everything pointed to the fact that Mary was unfaithful and now was pregnant!

If the situation was not bad enough, she had the gall to tell me that it was God who impregnated her. Thinking I had misheard, I asked her to repeat herself. She said, "God impregnated me."

I was livid! It was one thing to cheat and ask for forgiveness, that I could probably do, but she insisted that she had not been unfaithful and that there was nothing for me to forgive. What type of fool did she think I was? Rather than say what was in my heart, I walked away. What would you have done in my situation?

I aimlessly roamed for the rest of the day. There was a war in my head as thoughts and counter-thoughts collided with one other. Once my anger subsided, some modicum of reason started to kick in. She wasn't the Mary I knew or at least not the Mary I thought I knew. Where was the girl I had fallen in love with and was ready to marry?

I finally reasoned that someone bewitched her. Perhaps some evil deity had possessed her. I needed an explanation of what, why, and how it had happened outside of the spurious concocted nonsense that Mary had espoused just a few hours previously. Unable to find an answer that satisfied me, I decided that I had tortured myself long enough for the day and went to bed.

That's when it happened! A stunningly radiant figure appeared out of nowhere and called my name. With my mouth agape, I just stood in frozen silence. This figure, whom I now know was an angel from God called my name once more, and then began to speak. He spoke of Mary and repeated the very things that she had mentioned concerning the conception of the baby growing inside of her.

It turned out her words weren't some spurious concocted nonsense as I had thought, but the truth, the whole truth, and nothing but the truth. So, help her God.

If I had ended my relationship with her, I would have been doing her an injustice because she was innocent of the accusations, I levied against her. Furthermore, if I had walked away, I would have robbed myself of the opportunity to fulfill my life's God-ordained purpose. I woke up from my dream, grateful that I did not make a rash decision and knowing that the promise that lay ahead of me was worth the social pain we both would have to endure.

Relationship Lessons

1. It is better to respond to situations after much thought rather than react to circumstances out of emotions.
2. When someone does something that is out of their character, it is an invitation for you to dig deeper. Don't look at the 'what' but consider the 'why'.
3. Don't take any incident at face value; there is normally something deeper happening beneath the surface.
4. Sometimes the most beautiful things can blossom from the oddest and unplanned situations.
5. Don't be so quick to give up when your relationship turns belly up. Invite God into the circumstance and allow him to give you a unique perspective.

Meditation and Prayer

God uses the foolish things of this world to confound the wisdom of the wise. **– 1 Corinthians 1:27 –**

My precious Lord in all things who brings glory. Today, I lift my prayer to you confused. There are situations I find myself in that I don't understand. They are all around me, and I need Your guidance to comfort with a loving spirit and not have my feelings tainted. I pray that you give me discernment in all situations without me being judgmental. Allow me to understand that things aren't always what they seem and that there must be a deeper meaning; if not a lesson for me to learn. I know that You are wise, and I accept all that You have in store for me. In Jesus' name, I lift my confusion up to You so that I can do Your will to glorify Your name. Amen.

Life Application

How can you use the lessons learned in this chapter and apply it to your relationship? Meditate on your answer and lift up your specific prayer to God. He is faithful, and He will deliver.

Boaz
Look Beyond the Surface

The woman I ended up with would not have won The Most Likely to be Married contest. In fact, on the surface, she was no catch at all. If asked about whom you'd like to marry, I doubt you'd say, "I want a woman who is broke, destitute, poor, widowed, and who has a family history of incest and idolatry."

If those were not warning signs enough, her best friend was a bitter woman who had lost her zeal for life.

This was not the kind of history that most people would want you to know, much less confess. Yet, Ruth was not that way. She did not go around telling everyone her past, but she didn't try to cover it up either. That was intriguing to me!

See, I lived in a place where the utmost importance was placed on family history and lineage. In my society, it is natural to wear a mask and portray the good and hide away the bad. It was not only natural for people to keep up appearances, it was expected! Anyone not doing so was considered foolish.

I never liked the idea of keeping up appearances; it made for unreal and phony relationships. Relationships in which everyone performed for each other and where no one knew the other person seemed ludicrous. Ruth was not like everyone else. Given the social pressure she faced, that she shared her baggage, showed me that she was a confident woman who had made peace with her history.

So, I began to keep a watchful eye on her. The person I discovered when I got to know her defied her history. She was a loving, kind, industrious, resourceful, and strong woman who carried a deep sense of loyalty. With such character traits, I knew that she had a bright future ahead of her. I married her quickly.

It is often said that the greatest predictor of future behavior is past behavior. This is what leads to the saying, "Once a cheater, always a cheater." The problem with this stance is that it assumes that people do not change. This is not true. Since people change, it is both unfair and dangerous to label anyone solely based on their history. It is unfair to the person who has changed for the better because they will always be judged on something that they cannot go back and undo.

When I saw Ruth, I decided to focus my attention on who she was in the present and not who she was before. I also judged carefully to understand the attitude of her heart. I wanted to make sure that she had a high moral compass and was all in for God. The moment I validated her heart's attitude toward God and was satisfied with her character, I chose to forget her past.

Relationship Lessons

1. You will miss out on a great future if you are always looking at the past. Sometimes the best gifts do not come in the most attractive boxes.
2. A person's heart attitude toward God determines future behavior.
3. It is better to know and be known rather than keep up appearances.
4. Just because a person has done something wrong in the past does not mean they will repeat the same behavior in the future.
5. You must look beneath the surface to make the right relationship decision.

Meditation and Prayer

*In this new life, it doesn't matter if you are a Jew or a Gentile, circumcised or uncircumcised, barbaric, uncivilized, slave, or free. Christ is all that matters, and he lives in all of us. – **Colossians 3:11** –*

My Father, please hear my prayer. Thank you for accepting me as I am and forgiving me unconditionally for my past wrongs. You are a just and mighty God with the power to love and to teach us how to treat others. I pray that you give me the wisdom not to judge others for the past, but to accept them and allow them to show me the real them in Your presence. Just as you have forgiven me, I realize I need to forgive others too. I pray that my heart will be clean and that I can show Your love to others as You have showed Yours to me. Thank You for giving Your Son so that we may have eternal life. In all things good and merciful, I lift my requests to you. Amen.

Life Application

How can you use the lessons learned in this chapter and apply it to your relationship? Meditate on your answer and lift up your specific prayer to God. He is faithful, and He will deliver.

David
Do Not Marry for Security

When I got married, it was not because I loved my wife! Nope, love had nothing to do with it. I married her because I was afraid to disappoint her father. I married her for security! See, my first wife was the king's daughter. I was one of his loyal servants and warriors. Due to my prowess in battle, my fame and popularity had spread so much that the king became jealous of me. It got so bad that he saw me as a threat to his throne, although I did not desire to be king. To eliminate me as a threat, he attempted to kill me, but I escaped from his deadly hands. Seeing that killing me might not be the most popular move, he decided on a clever tactic and decided to give his daughter's hand to me in marriage.

He did this for three reasons. First, he could set a bride price, which I would have to honor, or I would be shamed. The bride price he set for me was to fight two hundred of the enemy troops alone. He set this gruesome and unusual bride price, knowing that the chances I would die were high. Second, he thought he could collude with his daughter to bring me harm, thinking that his daughter would be more faithful to him than she would to me. Third, if the other two tactics didn't work, he believed that the very nature of me being his son-in-law would secure my loyalty to him and reduce the chances of me wanting his throne.

I had already told him that I didn't desire to be married to his daughter using the excuse that I was not a worthy man. Yet, I caved into his request when he insisted. It was not that I couldn't say no. It was that I did not want the king as my enemy. I reasoned that he would not want to kill his son-in-law, especially one whom his daughter loved.

His daughter loved me greatly! I could see the twinkle in her eyes when she looked into mine. She not only loved me, she also respected me for my military prowess. She proved her love unequivocally when she warned me that her father had plotted to kill me. Not only did she warn me, she also let me out of a window at night and placed a dummy on the bed in my place to fool the men who had come to do that dastardly deed.

There was only one problem with our relationship. I didn't love her. I am ashamed to say it, but I didn't keep in touch with her after she helped me escape from the death wish of her father. Since she did not have my heart, I stopped trying to work on the relationship the moment she could not provide me the security I thought I would get by marrying her. Thinking there was no way this relationship would work, I married other women without divorcing her. This was cruel! If I didn't want her, I should have at least divorced her, so she would be free to marry again.

Her father, seeing that his tactic had not worked and that his daughter was stuck, decided to step in. Against Biblical law, he decided to give his daughter, my wife, to another man to marry to take away her shame as it was very shameful in those times for a man to abandon his wife.

Later, I decided to lay claim to her as my legal wife and bring her back to my home. You would have thought I did this because I realized it was wrong of me to abandon her. No! That was not it. I did it so I could use her as a pawn to win a peace treaty between me, the King of Judah, and the King of Israel who just happened to be her first cousin. I did it not because I wanted her back but because I wanted peace between her family and mine.

So, I married her for security, abandoned her for security, and took her back for security. Every decision I made regarding her was about what I could gain and never what I could give to her. Every decision concerning our relationship was born out of fear and selfishness.

When she came back to me, it was not because she wanted to. Although she respected my position as a king, she did not respect me as a person. The damage to our relationship was done.

So, I ask you, why are you looking to get married? Why are you looking to be in a relationship? Is it for what you can give, or is it for what you can gain?

Love always looks for what it can give to people but fear always looks for what it can get from people. What is driving you to marry? Is it the desire not to be alone? Is it for financial security? Is it for power?

Whatever you do, don't be like me! Don't use someone's heart as a pawn to gain what you desire. You will only leave that person hurt and bitter. Instead, be that person who marries for love, which means you are always looking to add value to your spouse and desire for them to experience the best life possible.

Relationship Lessons

1. A marriage based on what you can get will end up being an unhappy marriage.
2. If you do not love your spouse, you will abandon the marriage even if you are there physically.
3. Do not let your fear of the future lead you into a relationship.
4. Never enter or stay in a relationship because you are afraid to hurt someone's feeling. It is better to let the person know you do not feel the same than take them for a ride.
5. It is better to stay single until you know you can truly give love.

Meditation and Prayer

*A lying tongue hates its victims, and a flattering mouth works ruin. – **Proverbs 26:28** –*

Hear my prayer, Father, as I am in need of Your wisdom and guidance to allow me to search my heart for the truth in my relationship. Please help me to discern if I am making the right decision, and if I am, let Your will be done in me. Give me the strength to be honest and open in my relationship so that we may grow together and prosper in Your Love. In Jesus' name, I lift my requests to you knowing that You will provide for me now and in the future in all things. Amen.

Life Application

How can you use the lessons learned in this chapter and apply it to your relationship? Meditate on your answer and lift up your specific prayer to God. He is faithful, and He will deliver.

David
Set Boundaries

It was springtime; the time when kings regularly go out to battle. I was expected to do the same as I was the King. There was only one problem; I did not want to go into battle. I had been involved in several battles at this point, and I wanted to take a break from it all. Yet, I knew that not going to battle was political suicide.

If I didn't go out to war, it would make people question my credentials as their king. Worse, it would send the wrong message to the neighboring kings, who might think that I did not go to war because I was ill-prepared or that there was discord within the kingdom. If that happened, they would send their army to invade.

What was I to do? After pondering this for about a day, I decided to send out my army into battle, but I stayed home. Although my action was unusual, I saw it as accomplishing two purposes. First, it would solve the problem of putting the kingdom in jeopardy of being invaded. Second, I could tell the people that we were so superior to the other nations around us that I didn't need to be there in person. I could say that by me not being on the battlefield, we were projecting strength and force. Problem solved!

That spring, I went to battle, technically speaking, although I was not physically present. Instead of being on the field of battle, I languished around in the palace doing what I had planned to do, which was a whole lot of nothing. Then one day, I looked out from my palace into the city, and there in my line of sight was a beautiful woman bathing.

Instead of taking my eyes away, I decided to allow my eyes to linger. I justified my actions by saying to myself that all the other men do it. I convinced myself that it was okay to look if I did not touch and that I had done nothing wrong by looking. I was just being a guy, doing what every other guy would do if they saw a stunning woman bathing! The only problem was that I could not get her image out of my mind.

Now unable to get her out of my mind, I inquired about her. How unhappy I was when I found out she was married. I said to myself that she was off-limits. I let my mind wander away from having any relationship with her.

Being that her husband was fighting for me, I thought it reasonable to invite her over to the palace to let her know that her husband's sacrifice was not in vain. Here is how I justified my invitation: First, it would be a great honor for her to have an audience with the king. Second, by speaking well of her husband, she would be comforted and think even more highly of him. Third, it would make me feel better about spying on her as she bathed.

All my technicalities and justification left me the moment she walked into the palace. I knew I had lied to myself concerning my intentions and my ability to handle temptation. I knew I was in trouble! Instead of immediately sending her away, faking illness or inform her I had official business to attend, I proceeded to have the meeting. I told myself that I was strong enough to resist. I was not! I ended up taking her on a private tour of the palace. We were now past the point of no return. The private tour ended with a visit to my bedroom chamber.

I never took myself for someone who would cheat, but that was exactly what I ended up doing. When I look back, I see where I went wrong.

First, I abdicated my purpose and duty as a king. It is said that an idle mind is the devil's workshop. If you don't want to fall prey to various temptations, make sure you always keep your life goals and purpose in front of you. They have the quality of streamlining your life and keeping you out of trouble.

Second, I lived on the edge between right and wrong. It is said that if you live your life on the edge, it is only a matter of time until you fall off.

Third, I kept making excuses and justifying my behavior. It is easy to excuse and justify your decisions. To keep out of trouble, it is better to keep as many things as possible in the black or white category, for trouble follows those who live in the gray area.

Fourth, I compared myself to other people. Just because everybody was doing something does not mean I should do the same things. You can either choose to sink to the lowest standards or choose the highest standards. You can choose to be the best or choose to be just like the rest.

Relationship Lessons

1. You must set boundaries for yourself that you decide you won't cross.
2. If you live on the edge, it is only a matter of time until you fall off. Don't push your relationship boundaries.
3. When you let your eyes linger, it is easy for your thoughts and imagination to take over.
4. If you are not busy doing the right things, you are busy doing the wrong things. Focus on doing the right things, and the wrong things will disappear.
5. It is better for you to choose and set the standard for a relationship rather than to follow social norms.

Meditation and Prayer

They also learn to waste their time in going around from house to house; but even worse, they learn to be gossips and busybodies, talking of things they should not. – 1 Timothy 5:13 –

Lord, today I ask you to curb my tempting thoughts and behavior. It hasn't always been easy for me, but I know in my heart what is right and what is wrong. Please help me to remember Your Commandments as written in scripture and for me to apply them when temptation surfaces. Allow me to see that by following Your example, I can lead a fulfilled life free of temptation and bring glory to Your name. I ask you these things in Jesus' name. Amen.

Life Application

How can you use the lessons learned in this chapter and apply it to your relationship? Meditate on your answer and lift up your specific prayer to God. He is faithful, and He will deliver.

Leah
How to Survive a Stale Marriage

What do you do when your spouse no longer loves you? What do you do when he desires someone else? What do you when there is no emotional or physical intimacy? If you are going through these situations, then you probably feel rejected, worthless, and empty on the inside. I know how you feel because I was in a loveless marriage. I was a loveless woman where I was playing second fiddle to another woman, which brought me to think of myself as a failed woman.

For me, leaving the marriage was not an option. When I said, "For better or worse," on my wedding day, I meant it. I wasn't going to go back on those words and go back to living under my father's roof.

Since leaving was out of the question, I chose the only other thing I knew to do and fought for my marriage. I reasoned that my husband didn't have feelings for me because I wasn't meeting his needs. So, I paid extra attention to everything he liked and made sure I did everything exactly the way he liked it. I presented myself well, became a 'Yes' woman, and made sure I was always on my best behavior around him. When this didn't work, I reasoned that he didn't love me because I hadn't given birth to any children.

You should have seen how excited I was when I got pregnant. That excitement reached its crescendo when I gave birth to a baby boy. I knew he wanted a son. I named him Rueben, which means "See a Son." I thought for sure things would change in my marriage! Indeed, things did change for a while. My husband paid me a bit more attention, not to the level I desired, but better than before. Unfortunately, this didn't last long. He quickly reverted to his old ways, and I felt unloved once again.

Ever the fighter, I decided that I'd try once again to win his attention. Seeing that having a baby boy improved matters for a while, I prayed earnestly for another son. Then it happened again. I became pregnant and had another son. So, I called my son Simeon, which means "Heard." I was thankful for God for giving me another shot at saving my marriage by giving my husband another son. In a repeat of what previously occurred, the bond between my husband and I got stronger for a short while. Yet again, the bond was short-lived, and we reverted to being in a loveless marriage.

You would have thought I had learned my lesson by now. You would have thought I would have figured out that having babies would not restore the intimacy in my marriage. In hindsight, I think some part of me knew it, but I was not strong enough to admit it. So, when I had a third son, I reasoned that this would solidify the bond between my husband and me. I called him Levi, which means "Attached." You can guess what happened this third time. Yes, you guessed it. It did nothing to improve the intimacy in our marriage.

After this third go around, I decided to stop lying to myself. Although it hurt, I came to terms with the fact that there was nothing I could do to earn my husband's love. True love is not something that can be earned but is something that is freely given. I realized that I could not change my husband heart. That is only a feat that God can achieve. And, since God is a gentleman, he would not force my husband's heart to change toward me. That was my husband's choice.

I also came to realize that I too had a choice. I could continue to base my happiness on how my husband felt about me, or I could choose to base my happiness on how God felt about me. I could go through life mopping about what I did not have, or I could go through life focusing on the blessings I had. That is when things changed for me. Though my situation did not change, I changed!

I came to see my children as blessings from God. They loved me, accepted me, and desired to be around me. By the time I had my fourth son, I named him Judah, which means "Praise." This time, I was totally free to enjoy God's blessing in my life. I had gotten rid of all the expectations I had from my husband. I had rid myself of the shackle of performance. I had come to find my contentment in God.

So, how do you survive a stale and loveless marriage? The secret is to understand that your earthly husband is your second husband. So long as you are married to Christ, you will never be in a loveless marriage. Once you understand this, then it is up to you to open yourself to see the ways He is showing you love and to accept it. He is more than able to fill those areas of your life that are empty in His own unique way.

Relationship Lessons

1. Happiness comes from placing all your expectations on God.
2. When the circumstances of your relationship do not change, you must change.
3. No matter what your circumstance is, you get to choose what you focus on.
4. True love cannot be earned; it is freely given regardless of your performance.
5. So long as you are married to Christ, you will never be in a loveless marriage.

Meditation and Prayer

*The Lord is near to the brokenhearted and saves those who are crushed in spirit. **– Psalm 34:18 –***

Dear Lord, thank you for always being near me and to guide me. Although I stray when I'm frustrated or feel unloved, I know that you love me unconditionally. I pray that you surround me in your love so that I may receive and be blessed with true happiness in Your glory. Help me to accept that I can only change myself and not others and that my happiness is controlled within me. In Jesus' name, I lift my prayer to you. Amen.

Life Application

How can you use the lessons learned in this chapter and apply it to your relationship? Meditate on your answer and lift up your specific prayer to God. He is faithful and He will deliver.

Hosea
It's Not About You

Get away from me Devil was the first thought I uttered when a still-small voice told me that I should go to a prostitute and ask for her hand in marriage! Yet, I couldn't shake the words that the still-small voice spoke to me. What troubled me was that I recognized the still-small voice all too well. It was the voice of God.

I knew His voice very well because I was a prophet. My ministry began many years before, and I had a reputation for accurately predicting events before they happened. God told me everything I had predicted, and none of it ever failed to come to pass. So, when I heard His voice tells me to marry a prostitute, I knew it was Him speaking.

I heard it, but I didn't like it. I had many questions. How could I, a well-known and respected prophet, go and take a prostitute as a wife? This would be like Billy Graham deciding to go to a red-light district to choose his wife. I asked God many times if he was sure this was what he wanted me to do. I started to reason with Him. I said, "Lord, can You imagine the ridicule I will face? Everyone will think that I too, have neglected You and have decided to do whatever is in my heart. Lord, how can I be an effective witness when I choose a woman of the night?"

Then I started to think that maybe God was punishing me. I asked God if I had done something wrong. He told me, "No!" He told me that this marriage was a last-ditch multi-year effort to show my countrymen where they had gone astray. It was an attempt to save them for the justice and judgment that was going to be meted out to them if they did not change their ways. God was asking me to do this because he loved His people, and He knew I could handle it.

That is when I understood that this marriage was not about me. I realized I was more worried about my public image than I was in doing God's will. My blueprint for my life did not include marrying a prostitute, but His blueprint had it. I now had to decide if I was going to follow my blueprint, or was I going to follow God's? That was a huge decision.

When it comes to choosing a partner, God may not be as extreme with you as He was with me. Yet, He wants you to know that marriage is not about you but is designed to accomplish a higher purpose – His purpose. So, ask yourself this, "Am I willing to do what God asks of me, or am I too concerned about what society will think?"

What does that look like for you? Is it marrying somebody from a different culture? Is it marrying someone who has a different shade of color? What is stopping you from doing what God is asking you to do?

After much pouting and prayer, I decided to do what God asked. I took Gomer as my wife. I said to myself, "I know what God will do. He will turn Gomer around, and she will be faithful to me. He will use the turnaround to show the people that they are not too far gone; that they also can change their ways before it is too late."

What a testimony if the relationship played out the way I thought about it.

It was a nice story I convinced myself about, but it was all wishful thinking. Gomer didn't change at all. In fact, she used the fact that she knew I would always do the will of God to commit adultery freely. She was secure in the knowledge that I was not going to divorce her. I am telling you this part of my story to let you know that just because you obey God doesn't mean everything will go smoothly. It doesn't mean that the person you marry will change.

Like Gomer, the person you are with may take your faithfulness to God as foolishness. Just because you have done all the right things, you prayed to God, stayed pure, committed your heart, and have chosen to love, doesn't mean you will have a successful marriage. No matter how good you are, your partner has a choice on how they will behave. Don't take on the burden of changing your partner because it can't be done.

If I had taken Gomer's adulterous behavior as a verdict on how well I was doing as a husband, I would have been depressed. All I could do was follow God, love her, and pray for her. Whether she yielded her heart to God was her choice.

Relationship Lessons

1. Your marriage is not about you. It is about fulfilling a purpose greater than yourself.
2. Just because you obey God perfectly, doesn't mean everything in your marriage will be perfect. Your partner still has their free will.
3. You did not marry your spouse to change them; you married your spouse to love them.
4. Your love should not hinge on the performance of your spouse but should always be measured by your obedience to God.
5. You are not responsible for your spouse's behavior; you are responsible only for your own behavior.

Meditation and Prayer

*But to those of you who will listen, I say: Love your enemies, do good to those who hate you, bless those who curse you, pray for those who mistreat you. – **Luke 6:27 – 28***

My precious Jesus, I know that I can be self-centered and think that things are always about me. It is selfish for me to think this and I need Your help to overcome. Help me to recognize my errors and take responsibility for my actions. When others offend me, give me the strength and wisdom to turn my cheek and pray for them. Also, allow me to recognize that I don't have the ability to change anyone other than myself. I lift these things up to You in Jesus's name. Amen.

Life Application

How can you use the lessons learned in this chapter and apply it to your relationship? Meditate on your answer and lift up your specific prayer to God. He is faithful and He will deliver.

Job
Choose Wisely

How many times have you heard, "For better or worse, for richer or poorer, in sickness and in heath, 'til death do us part?" This is the classical vow that many couples recite on their wedding day. My wedding day was no different although we didn't use those exact words. As time passed, God blessed us more than we could ever have imagined, and we lived a very luxurious life.

Then one day, seemingly out of nowhere, we lost it all. This was a very dark and painful period in our lives, and it shook us to our very core. No one knows what a man is made of until he is squeezed. It has been said that adversity introduces a man to himself. In my case, adversity introduced me to a woman who was different from the wife I thought I knew.

Somewhere along the way, she let the riches we amassed get to her head. She began to trust in our wealth more than she trusted in God. In fact, it turned out that her love for God was based solely on what He could do for her. I know all this because after we lost it all, she told me to curse God!

She forgot that God owns everything, therefore, she elevated us to the position of owners instead of stewards. She also forgot that there is nothing that is lost that God cannot restore. She forgot that during times of trouble are the times we need to lean on God more than ever, for only He has the power to save and restore.

I also learned during that time that she didn't love me for me, but she loved me for what I could provide her. I thought she respected me for being a man of integrity, a man who stayed the course and does not waiver in his convictions, a man who is rooted and ground in God, and a man not easily shaken. Yet, when we lost it all, she mocked me for holding onto my integrity. She asked me what good was my integrity if all the calamity still befell me.

I was shocked when I heard that. I thought she liked who I was. I believed that she understood the person I was, had a big hand in helping us achieve the status we reached. She was now insinuating that my integrity had nothing to do with it. In a sense, she rejected who I was because the circumstances of our lives drastically changed. I saw that she had lost all respect for me.

The vows she took on our wedding day meant nothing to her. She said them with her mouth but did not cherish them in her heart. I learned this when she told me that I should just die! See, at that time, it was unusual for a woman to divorce a man. Hence, the only other way for a woman to leave a marriage was if her husband died. By saying I should just die, what she was saying was that she didn't want to be married any longer. If I died, someone else could take care of her.

The scales fell off my eyes. She didn't consider my condition but only thought of herself. I realized she was not a strong woman as she could not handle the challenges life threw her. It dawned on me that she was not a woman of faith. I came to see that her commitment to me was conditional. Somehow, I had missed the warning signs before we married.

So, I tell you, before you get married you want to make sure that your partner has a personal relationship with God. This means you shouldn't be the one having to drag them to church. You shouldn't be the one asking to read the *Bible* and asking for them to pray.

Moreover, you want to see how they handle little-life troubles. If they get frustrated over every little thing; if every molehill looks like a mountain in their eyes, then they won't be able to handle the bigger issues of life, unless they grow in the knowledge of God and yield their hearts to Him. So, I beg you, choose wisely.

Relationship Lessons

1. Make sure the person you marry has their own personal relationship with God.
2. A person who makes mountains out of molehills is likely unable to deal with a real mountain.
3. Wealth makes you incredibly attractive, so make doubly sure your partner is attracted to you more than what you have.

4. When in the middle of a storm, be sure to lean heavily on God, for those you think should have your back may not be of much help.

Meditation and Prayer

*Charm is deceitful, and beauty is vain, but a woman who fears the Lord, she will be praised. – **Proverbs 31:30** –*

My dear Lord, guide me to be the best possible steward of the earthly possessions You have gifted me. May I treasure heavenly thoughts over earthly thoughts. I pray that when I choose my life partner that they too will walk in Your Glory and have a personal relationship with you so that we may do Your will and praise your name. Amen.

Life Application

How can you use the lessons learned in this chapter and apply it to your relationship? Meditate on your answer and lift up your specific prayer to God. He is faithful and He will deliver.

Samson
Avoid This Mistake When Choosing

If you're considering choosing a life partner, then you want to concern yourself with my story. While it will not tell you what to do, it will show you what you shouldn't do.

See, I had a problem with women! I loved them all. Long hair, short hair, slender, athletic, full-bodied, dark, light; none of that mattered to me. I loved them all. One day as I walked down the street corner in a neighborhood that belonged to the Philistines, I saw a beautiful woman from the corner of my eye. Being the kind of guy that takes a second look, I stopped and stared at her. It was love at first sight. I knew right then that I wanted her to be my wife.

That was my first mistake. I believed in love at first sight. I made my decision on the person to marry based solely on her physical appearance. I knew absolutely nothing about this woman. I knew nothing of her reputation or her character. Yet, within a few minutes of seeing her, I had made up my mind to marry her. I made my decision based on chemical impulses.

Love is a commitment. Within the context of a romantic relationship, you can't have a commitment at the first sight of seeing the person you believe you want to marry. The best thing you can hope for is connection, chemistry, and compassion. For me, it wasn't love at first sight; it was lust at first sight.

Convinced that I loved her, I went home and told my parents about my intentions to marry her. Being wise parents, they warned me that I would be unequally yoked to her if I chose to marry her. They begged me to find someone who had the same morals, values, and belief system as me. Foolishly, I told them that all of that did not matter. After all, I was in love!

"In love," my mother repeated. "What do you love about her?"

Knowing that I did not know her well, I stormed out of the room and pretended the conversation never happened.

That was my second mistake. I shied away from having the tough, but necessary, conversations concerning my choices with those whom I knew loved me. I failed to heed the advice of those whom I knew had godly wisdom. See, when in the throes of emotion, your feelings take over to such an extent that you fail to see danger signs. In those times, you see only what you want to see, and what you want to see is only the good things in life. If you're going to make the right decisions about whom to partner with, then you need to bring in those who love you enough to give you their honest and godly prayerful thoughts.

When the week to celebrate the marriage came, I decided I was going to post a riddle to her kinsmen. If they could tell me the meaning of the riddle, I would give them substantial amounts of expensive clothing, but if they couldn't, then they would have to buy me lots of clothes. Her kinsmen, not wanting to spend a fortune on clothing, threatened her life if she did not find out the meaning of the riddle from me in advance of the challenge.

Think about that for a minute? What kind of kinsmen threatens the life of their family member during their marriage celebration? What kind of kinsmen places money above life? I think that was my third mistake. I did not think!

When I did tell her the meaning of the riddle, she told her kinsmen, and I ended up giving them the clothes I promised. It wasn't losing the bet that hurt me. It was the fact that my wife felt a deeper sense of loyalty to her kinsmen than she did to me, her husband. Furthermore, I realized that my wife did not trust me to protect her. She knew how strong I was and that no one could stand up to me. Yet, she decided to go behind my back.

Before you choose a partner, you must make sure that the person is ready to leave her family and cleave to you. It doesn't mean that you treat the family like outsiders or outlaws, although some in-laws behave more like outlaws. Leaving means that there is a switch in loyalty. Without this loyalty switch, real trust can't be built. Without trust, your marriage will not thrive. It is that simple. With broken trust, my marriage not only did not thrive, but it also did not survive.

So, I warn you. Take these lessons from my life about choosing a spouse and don't end up like me – jumping around from partner to partner and ruining my life in the process.

Relationship Lessons

1. Do not be unequally yoked with a person that has different morals, values, belief systems.
2. Make sure you ask for the honest and godly thoughts and opinions of wise people in your life.
3. Do not base your choice solely on appearance, for appearance fades.
4. There is no such thing as love at first sight, only connection, chemistry, and possibly compassion at first sight.
5. You cannot afford divided loyalties if trust is to be built in a marriage.

Meditation and Prayer

*But you shall go to my country and to my family and take a wife for my son Isaac. – **Genesis 24:4** –*

Dear Lord, hear my prayer of trust and honesty. I know that deception is from the devil's hands and not Yours. I pray that I find the courage to deny evil doings and not choose a partner not yoked in Your word and not covered in Your grace. I pray that I choose wisely a person who is honest and shares the same values and beliefs as I do that is grounded in Your word. I ask these things in Jesus' name so that I may please you and do your will. Amen.

Life Application

How can you use the lessons learned in this chapter and apply it to your relationship? Meditate on your answer and lift up your specific prayer to God. He is faithful and He will deliver.

Vashti
Involve God and Wait on God's Timing

I was shocked when I heard that Queen Esther went into the King's chambers without being invited. What! That itself was an offense punishable by death. Yet, King Xerxes didn't commit her to the gallows or at a minimum remove her as his Queen. Why did Xerxes show Esther favor when she broke his law but didn't even hear my words when I broke his law?

See, before Esther became queen, I was Xerxes wife. I was the Queen of the land. In that time, women were treated as second-hand subjects of the kingdom. However, I didn't experience much of this when I was growing up. I was the great-granddaughter of a king. My father treated me with as much respect as he could, but things changed when the Persians took over the kingdom, and I was given to Xerxes.

I was tired of being treated like a woman whose sole purpose in life was to do the whim and whams of her husband. So, when Xerxes summoned me to come and parade myself in front of his princes, like some sort of an object, I refused! I saw it as demeaning and unnecessary. It was a calculated risk I took that day. I knew I was the only woman in the kingdom who was in a position to stand up for women's rights. First, being an heir of the old beloved Babylonian king and revered by the people of the land, I knew it was unlikely for Xerxes to call for my death. It would be too risky a call to make. Second, if my defiance worked, it had the power to set millions of women free of their husband's control.

Unfortunately, my plans backfired, and I ended up being removed as queen. At the time, I was confused. I had been taught as a child, by learned men who served God, that men and women were equal under the sight of God. I was taught that God was not a respecter of persons.

I knew this to be true when I heard the stories of how Daniel and his friends defied my great-grandfather and suffered no consequence. Although I did not know God personally, I thought this as something that God would desire! I had questions. Why did God honor Esther's desire to save her people from destruction, but He didn't honor my desire to save women from men's oppression? Did God desire for women to continue to be oppressed and repressed?

You may have the same questions. Why do things sometimes go awry when you take a stand for what is right? When is it okay to challenge your husband's leadership?

When I studied why Esther was successful in her bid, and I was not, I came to realize a few things. First, Esther sought wise counsel and prayer before she took any action. I did not! Although my heart's desire was right, I didn't check with God to ensure my timing was right. King Solomon wrote in his book that a man's heart plans his way, but the Lord directs his steps. I didn't allow God to direct my steps. I planned what I wanted to do, but I didn't seek God to tell me when and how to do it.

Second, Esther defied Xerxes in the privacy of the palace. I defied the king in public. In private, Xerxes was my husband, the king. But in public, he was the king, who just happened to be my husband. If I had taken a stand in private, he would have had the opportunity to respond as my husband and not the king of the land. He then could have changed laws as the king because of his heart change as a husband. By taking a stand in public, I gave him no choice but to respond as a king first. I had disrespected him in public. What was I thinking?

If I could do it over again, I would have done it differently. I would have waited for the right time and the right setting. I would have sought out godly counsel and instruction. Then I would have prayed before broaching the topic with Xerxes.

If you have a difficult topic that you need to bring up to your spouse, consider these same steps that Esther took. You will increase your chances of success!

Relationship Lessons

1. It isn't enough to have the right intentions. You must go about achieving your right intentions in the right way to get the right results.

2. Don't rush into anything. Wait on God's timing and God's setting.
3. Always seek godly counsel and instruction before broaching a difficult subject with your spouse.
4. It is okay to plan what you want to do, but make sure you involve God in prayer so He can direct your steps.
5. Do not bring your private issues into the public eye; it will only complicate matters.

Meditation and Prayer

*Commit your works to the LORD, and your thoughts will be established. – **Proverbs 16:3** –*

In the name of Jesus, I pray that I always seek your guidance and counsel in all things. When I do things on my own, I make grave mistakes and rush into things haphazardly. I pray that You grant me favor when I seek Your word in scripture and from the advice of wise elders whom I trust. Thank you for being a merciful God with wisdom beyond my imagination and gifting me with Your love and forgiveness. In all things, I pray and trust in Your word as it is true today, tomorrow, and for eternity. In Jesus' name, I present to you my prayer. Amen.

Life Application

How can you use the lessons learned in this chapter and apply it to your relationship? Meditate on your answer and lift up your specific prayer to God. He is faithful and He will deliver.

Solomon
Do Not Tolerate What is Wrong

I was young when I became a king. To be honest with you, it was a scary time for me because my father had many enemies who had their eyes on the throne. My brother made it clear he wanted to be the king over me. Being young, inexperienced, without a father, and feeling overwhelmed, I decided to go to the only person I knew could help me. I went to God in prayer.

In those early days, I had a humble and teachable heart. I asked for wisdom, and God gave it to me. I was so wise that many people came from foreign kingdoms to hear me speak. It was not long before I became extraordinarily prosperous and became extremely popular amongst the nations, which not only gave me the attention I wanted, but it also gave me the attention I would rather have avoided.

One of the attentions I did not ask for was the attention of worldly women. Going against God's instruction, I surrounded myself with many such women.

It was not long until I decided to marry one that did not believe in God. I justified it by saying this to myself, "I am the wisest person in the world. I am too wise to allow a non-believer to change my views about God."

Bam! Just like I thought, she didn't change my views about God. This made me bold. So, I decided to surround myself with more worldly women.

For many years there seemed to be no consequence attached to my disobedience. Therefore, I reasoned that God's instruction not to marry worldly women was for people whose hearts were not fully committed to Him.

I reasoned that since I was committed to God, instead of my heart turning away from Him, the women's hearts would turn toward the Holy One! I became wise in my own eyes and became prideful.

What I didn't realize was that by tolerating the idols these women brought into my life, I left an open door to rebellion against God. I dragged my relationship with God to the edge and left no room for error.

I fell off that edge in my old age. I finally rebelled against God after years of disobedience, lowering my guard. I knew I didn't have anyone to blame but myself. I tolerated the things I knew were wrong. I let my lustful desire to overcome my wisdom.

When it comes to your relationship, do not allow yourself to falter from God's instructions. Stay away from temptation and do not bring it home with you. I started well, but I didn't finish that way. Don't be like me.

Relationship Lessons

1. You are truly wise when you understand that there is One wiser than you.
2. The mess you tolerate in your relationship will make your relationship messy in the end.
3. Don't play with fire in your relationship; otherwise, you will get burned.
4. Do not invite temptation into your relationship.
5. Popularity and prosperity attract all type of people to you. Be careful which ones you invite into your life.

Meditation and Prayer

Do not be wise in your own eyes. **– Proverbs 3:7 –**

My dear Lord, I acknowledge that you are the Holy One who knows everything. Your wisdom surpasses all. I pray that in all decisions and in all my relationships that I rely on Your strength and example and turn to wise counsel. When it comes to my relationship, I pray that You grant me wisdom to do what is right so that I may bring glory to Your name and do Your will. I also pray that I receive strength to avoid lust and temptation as I am to cleave to my partner in love and cherish that relationship and not do anything to bring harm. Thank you for loving me and showing me what true love is. I lift my prayer to you as your humble servant. Amen.

Life Application

How can you use the lesson learned in this chapter and apply it to your relationship? Meditate on your answer and lift up your specific prayer to God. He is faithful and He will deliver.

Rachel
No One Can Make You Happy

How many of you can say that your man pursued you for fourteen years? I don't know about you, but I didn't think it was possible until it happened to me. My husband loved me so much that he was willing to work fourteen years to pay my bride price.

My marriage was great. He showered me with a lot of love and attention. There was nothing he withheld from me; yet, I was not happy. I looked at my sister and saw how many kids she had and became envious. Instead of looking at what I had, I was solely focused on what I didn't have.

The funny thing was my sister was also unhappy. Although she had lots of kids, she was envious of me because my husband loved me. She had what I wanted, and I had what she wanted! Oh my, what tangled webs we weave. We were both unhappy because we didn't have what we desired.

I never came to realize that happiness is not based on circumstance but based on perspective. My sister and I lost our perspective of our blessings because we focused on what we didn't have.

While my sister, Leah, ended up becoming happy with what she had, my outcome was a different story. I looked to control my circumstances until the very end. Therefore, I was unhappy during the full length of my marriage.

For me, the end came during childbirth. I was so happy that I was going to have the child I desired so much. I knew that my child would make me happy, but I had complications during childbirth. At that moment I said something I thought I would never say. Instead of one of the strong names I had been thinking about, I named my baby Benoni, which means "Son of my sorrow." Do you see it? I was saying to my son that I lived a sorrowful life because he didn't come into the world sooner, and now I leave this life not having experienced happiness.

I blamed everything and everyone for my unhappiness, and I was only going to be happy if I got what I wanted. If you are like me, let me tell you, you won't get everything you want in life, or at least not when you want it. You have a choice of what you are going to do in the waiting seasons. Will you be happy, or will you be sad? Will you focus on what you have, or will you focus on what you don't have?

No one can make you happy, but you. If you choose to focus on what you have instead of what you don't have, you will find yourself happier and enjoying life.

Bonus Relationship Lessons

1. Just because you have the perfect partner does not mean you will be happy.
2. You will be happy if you stop trying to control everything and stop trying to have your own way.
3. Happiness is not based on your circumstance, but on your perspective.

Meditation and Prayer

*You will make known to me the path of life; In Your presence is fullness of joy; In Your right hand there are pleasures forever. -**Psalm 16:11**-*

My dear and sweet Lord, I thank you for the joy and love You bring to my life for my happiness is found within You. Please help me to realize that I can't control other people's happiness and charge me with the responsibility of my own. I recognize that my happiness rests in my joy in loving You. I pray that I always see the good in life and in my partner and that I spread Your happiness and joy to others. I pray with the joy in my heart of loving You. Amen.

Life Application

How can you use the lesson learned in this chapter and apply it to your relationship? Meditate on your answer and lift up your specific prayer to God. He is faithful and He will deliver.

Summary of Lessons

I hope you have enjoyed reading and meditating on these lessons as narrated by each of the Biblical characters. To make it easier for you to review the lessons, I have organized them for you. One way you can best benefit from these is to write each one on a sticky note, once a week, and let it serve as your mantra. Review them often and pray on how you can improve your relationship with God and your partner.

1. Never sacrifice permanent joy for temporary gratification – the taste is not worth the pain.
2. God knows what is best for your relationship – always listen to Him and obey the commands He has for you.
3. You must let go of the past wrongs to move forward in your relationship with God and with your future or current spouse.

4. Your commitment to God will bolster your commitment to your partner
5. Your relationship will be exceptional if you are both committed to God in all things and remain faithful to His will and plans for you both.
6. Don't take your relationship with God for granted.
7. Maintain an attitude of gratitude; it will keep you from a lot of trouble.
8. Accept responsibility for your mess-ups instead of trying to justify them or blame them on others.
9. Look for and pay attention to the wise counsel of others.
10. Any decision you make when you're angry and frustrated will only hurt you and your relationship.
11. Look to live in community with one another instead of in competition.
12. For your relationship to last, you must look past what is wrong with your partner and instead focus on what is right with your partner.
13. It is not a matter of if you must forgive each other, it is a matter of when you must forgive.
14. Being disappointed in any relationship is inevitable but being discouraged is a choice.
15. Fear makes terrible relationship decisions, so never make any decisions out of fear.
16. Keep your focus on God's promises when going through a rough patch.
17. You are setting yourself up for a rude awakening if you expect you or your partner never to change.
18. The key to maintaining your relationship is making sure you change together.

19. It is not enough that you love each other; it is vital that you share the same vision for your lives. Having two visions leads to division.
20. It is better, to be honest, and truthful at the start rather than go along with something you know you can't handle.
21. Make sure you fix any serious issues you may have before introducing any major life changes.
22. Do not compromise your values – if you can't find what you are looking for in one place, expand your search. Do not limit yourself to one country, one ethnicity, one culture.
23. Do not yoke yourself to anyone that does not belong to your spiritual family.
24. Do not make the goal of being married more important than obeying God – any marriage that takes you away from fulfilling your purpose and destiny should be avoided.
25. Ask God for favor, wisdom, and spiritual eyes to see before choosing a potential spouse.
26. Do not delay in making a move when you see someone you like & do not delay putting 'a ring on it' when you know that person is the one for you.
27. Marry only when you are ready – It is better to be married later in life than to marry early and have a miserable marriage that ends in divorce.
28. Settle only for a quality spouse – No matter how many men and women there are, you will be with only one. Hearing a lot of 'no's' does not mean you are on the wrong track.

29. Be open to the person God desires for you. Having an idea of the person you desire to be with is fine but be open to the possibility of God moving you in a different direction.
30. Married life is not always a bouquet of flowers. Just because you are in the will of God does not mean everything in your marriage will go smoothly.
31. No waiting period is ever wasted. God always has a lesson in the waiting period. Look for it.
32. Pray and be patient through your troubles. When issues do pop up, remain prayerful, and ask God to grant you the wisdom to know how to wait. Delay is not denial.
33. Don't allow the things you can't do anything about stop you from pursuing your desire to marry. When the right person comes along, he won't care about things such as whether you were previously married, have kids, how old you are, etc.
34. Not every person is comfortable pursuing a relationship. If you are interested, you may have to make the first sure move.
35. There is no full-proof process to follow to get into a relationship and get married. The most important thing is to make sure that you choose wisely.
36. If you desire to be married, make sure you put your best foot forward. Moreover, remember this, if things don't work out, that there is no such thing as rejection, there is only redirection.
37. Sometimes you must break with culture and traditions to get what you desire. Don't let those stop you if you are not breaking God's commandments.

38. Love is not about getting your needs met first, it is first about meeting the needs of your partner.
39. When you say, "I love you," to someone, you should mean, "I selflessly sacrifice to serve you."
40. Love is not a feeling; love is an action.
41. Love is a gift given based on the heart of the giver and not a reward given based on the performance of the receiver.
42. Love is a committed expression to others of the love we have received from God.
43. Give people a chance to love you because you are worthy just the way you are to be loved.
44. Don't disqualify yourself from love prematurely because of the stories you have told yourself.
45. Your good character toward people forges loyalty in their relationship with you.
46. Who you are as a person is more important to people compared to what you may or may not have.
47. The people that love you will not abandon you in your time of trouble.
48. You must think for yourself instead of allowing your fears to think for you.
49. It is important to take a deliberate break to truly consider the other person's point of view.
50. You should consider both your head and heart when deciding. If you only allow your head to rule, it will take you to a place where your heart feels empty.
51. To make your partner more comfortable, give yourself an alternative solution in the event whatever decision you make does not work so well.

52. If you respond when you are -- Frustrated, Angry, Upset, Lonely, or Tired (F.A.U.L.T), then you are equally at fault for the argument.
53. It is better to respond to situations after much thought rather than react to circumstances out of emotions.
54. When someone does something that is out of their character, it is an invitation for you to dig deeper. Don't look at the 'what' but consider the 'why'.
55. Don't take any incident at face value; there is normally something deeper happening beneath the surface.
56. Sometimes the most beautiful things can blossom from the oddest and unplanned situations.
57. Don't be so quick to give up when your relationship turns belly up. Invite God into the circumstance and allow him to give you a distinct perspective.
58. You will miss out on a great future if you are always looking at the past. Sometimes the best gifts do not come in the most attractive boxes.
59. A person's heart attitude toward God determines future behavior.
60. It is better to know and be known rather than keep up appearances.
61. Just because a person has done something wrong in the past does not mean they will repeat the same behavior in the future.
62. You must look beneath the surface to make the right relationship decision.
63. A marriage based on what you can get will end up being an unhappy marriage.

64. If you do not love your spouse, you will abandon the marriage even if you are there physically.
65. Do not let your fear of the future lead you into a relationship.
66. Never enter or stay in a relationship because you are afraid to hurt someone's feelings. It is better to let the person know you do not feel the same than take them for a ride.
67. It is better to stay single until you know you can truly give love.
68. You must set boundaries for yourself that you decide you won't cross.
69. If you live on the edge, it is only a matter of time until you fall off. Don't push your relationship boundaries.
70. When you let your eyes linger, it is easy for your thoughts and imagination to take over.
71. If you are not busy doing the right things, you are busy doing the wrong things. Focus on doing the right things, and the wrong things will disappear.
72. It is better for you to choose and set the standard for a relationship rather than to follow social norms.
73. Happiness comes from placing all your expectations on God.
74. When the circumstances of your relationship do not change, you must change.
75. No matter what your circumstance is, you get to choose what you focus on.
76. True love cannot be earned; it is freely given regardless of your performance.

77. So long as you are married to Christ, you will never be in a loveless marriage.
78. Your marriage is not about you. It is about fulfilling a purpose greater than yourself.
79. Just because you obey God perfectly, doesn't mean everything in your marriage will be perfect. Your partner still has their free will.
80. You did not marry your spouse to change them; you married your spouse to love them.
81. Your love should not hinge on the performance of your spouse but should always be measured by your obedience to God.
82. You are not responsible for your spouse's behavior; you are responsible only for your own behavior.
83. Make sure the person you marry has their own personal relationship with God.
84. A person who makes mountains out of molehills is likely unable to deal with a real mountain.
85. Wealth makes you incredibly attractive, so make doubly sure your partner is attracted to you more than what you have.
86. When in the middle of a storm, be sure to lean heavily on God, for those you think should have your back may not be of much help.
87. Do not be unequally yoked with a person that has different morals, values, belief systems.
88. Make sure you ask for the honest and godly thoughts and opinions of wise people in your life.

89. Do not base your choice solely on appearance, for appearance fades.
90. There is no such thing as love at first sight, only connection, chemistry, and possibly compassion at first sight.
91. You cannot afford divided loyalties if trust is to be built in a marriage.
92. It isn't enough to have the right intentions. You must go about achieving your right intentions in the right way to get the right results.
93. Don't rush into anything. Wait on God's timing and God's setting.
94. Always seek godly counsel and instruction before broaching a difficult subject with your spouse.
95. It is okay to plan what you want to do, but make sure you involve God in prayer so He can direct your steps.
96. Do not bring your private issues into the public eye; it will only complicate matters.
97. You are truly wise when you understand that there is One wiser than you.
98. The mess you tolerate in your relationship will make your relationship messy in the end.
99. Don't play with fire in your relationship; otherwise, you will get burned.
100. Do not invite temptation into your relationship.
101. Popularity and prosperity attract all type of people to you. Be careful which ones you invite into your life.

Bonus Relationship Lessons

1. Just because you have the perfect partner does not mean you will be happy.
2. You will be happy if you stop trying to control everything and stop trying to have your own way.
3. Happiness is not based on your circumstance, but on your perspective.

Summary of Scriptures

Scriptures serve as a reminder of God's promises to us. Each scripture I chose throughout the book resonated with me on how we can improve our relationship with our partners and ourselves. Listed below are those scriptures. Review them often, reflect on each one at a time, and pray and allow God to transform you and bless your relationship. Also, you might want to write one down each week on an index card and memorize it. Carry it with you so that you may grow in His will and bring glory to His name.

- ➤ *Trust in the LORD with all your heart, and do not rely on your own understanding* – **Proverbs 3:5** –

- ➤ *If you become angry, do not let your anger lead you into sin, and do not stay angry all day.* – **Ephesians 4:26** –

- *If we are faithless, He remains faithful; He cannot deny Himself.* **– 2 Timothy 2:13 –**

- *Can two walk together, unless they are agreed?* **– Amos 3:3–**

- *Don't become partners with those who do not believe. For what partnership is there between righteousness and lawlessness? Or what fellowship does light have with darkness?* **– 2 Corinthians 6:14 –**

- *Be still and know that I am God.* **– Psalm 46:10 –**

- *Who are you? he asked. "It's Ruth, sir," she answered. Because you are a close relative, you are responsible for taking care of me. So please marry me.* **– Ruth 3:9 –**

- *For God so loved the world that He gave His only Begotten Son that whosoever believes in Him should not perish but have everlasting life.* **– John 3:16 –**

- *For as he (a man) thinks in his heart, so is he.* **– Proverbs 23:7 –**

- *A man's heart plans his way, but the Lord directs his steps* **– Proverbs 16:9 –**

- *God uses the foolish things of this world to confound the wisdom of the wise.* **– 1 Corinthians 1:27 –**

- In this new life, it doesn't matter if you are a Jew or a Gentile, circumcised or uncircumcised, barbaric, uncivilized, slave, or free. Christ is all that matters, and he lives in all of us. **– Colossians 3:11 –**

- A lying tongue hates its victims, and a flattering mouth works ruin. **– Proverbs 26:28 –**

- They also learn to waste their time in going around from house to house; but even worse, they learn to be gossips and busybodies, talking of things they should not. **– 1 Timothy 5:13 –**

- The Lord is near to the brokenhearted and saves those who are crushed in spirit. **– Psalm 34:18 –**

- But to those of you who will listen, I say: Love your enemies, do good to those who hate you, bless those who curse you, pray for those who mistreat you. **– Luke 6:27 – 28**

- Charm is deceitful, and beauty is vain, but a woman who fears the Lord, she will be praised. **– Proverbs 31:30 –**

- But you shall go to my country and to my family, and take a wife for my son Isaac. **– Genesis 24:4 –**

- Commit your works to the LORD, and your thoughts will be established. **– Proverbs 16:3 –**

➢ *Do not be wise in your own eyes. **– Proverbs 3:7 –***

➢ *You will make known to me the path of life; In Your presence is fullness of joy; In Your right hand there are pleasures forever. **-Psalm 16:11-***

About the Author

Emmanuel Ogunjumo, the founder of Relationship Minibooks, has studied all aspects of relationships relentlessly. He pursued this path of study after multiple failed relationships led him to humble himself and recommit to God. After several years of study, he has now committed himself to share all that he knows and continues to learn with those who have a desire to have high-quality relationships. Emmanuel strongly believes that relationships are not just meant to survive; they are meant to thrive. His desire is to change lives by putting an end to family separations, emotional turmoil, mental anguish, and financial woes created by failed relationships.

As an international speaker, author of five books including *D.E.A.R. Singles*, he serves as a relationship coach, a church board member and earned a Theology and Biblical Studies degree. He is happily married and lives in Houston, Texas.

CONTACT THE AUTHOR

Official Website: www.relationshipminibooks.com

Email: Emmanuel@relationshipminibooks.com

Emmanuel Ogunjumo

Notes

www.ingramcontent.com/pod-product-compliance
Lightning Source LLC
LaVergne TN
LVHW041340080426
835512LV00006B/543